HOCKEY CROSSWORDS

T.R. GRADY

ALL HOCKEY-RELATED CLUES AND ANSWERS: MORE THAN 900 CLUES

Published by Dylanna Press an imprint of Dylanna Publishing, Inc.
Copyright © 2022 by Dylanna Press

Author: T. R. Grady

All rights reserved. No part of this publication may be reproduced, stored in a retrieval system, or transmitted by any means, including electronic, mechanical, photocopying, or otherwise, without prior written permission of the publisher.

Limit of liability/Disclaimer of Warranty: The Publisher and the author make no representations or warranties with respect to the accuracy or completeness of the contents of this work and specifically disclaim all warranties, including without limitation warranties of fitness for a particular purpose.

Although the publisher has taken all reasonable care in the preparation of this book, we make no warranty about the accuracy or completeness of its content and, to the maximum extent permitted, disclaim all liability arising from its use.

This book is not endorsed by and is not associated with National Hockey League.

Trademarks: Dylanna Press is a registered trademark of Dylanna Publishing, Inc. and may not be used without written permission.

Puzzle #1

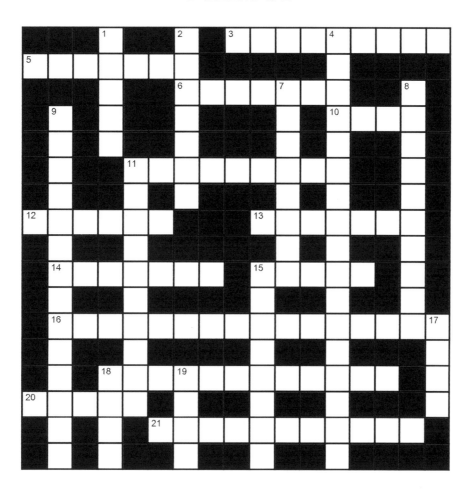

Across

- **3** 2022 Conn Smythe winner (4,5)
- **5** Panthers (7)
- **6** Arizona (7)
- **10** Curtis Joseph nickname (4)
- **11** Wrote rules for modern ice hockey (9)
- **12** 1969 Conn Smythe, MTL, Serge _____ (6)
- **13** 2003 Conn Smythe ANA, Jean-Sebastien _____ (7)
- **14** Islanders (3,4)
- **15** 1944 NHL MVP, TOR, Babe _____ (5)
- **16** St. Louis arena (10,6)
- **18** Little Ball of Hate, Bruins (4,8)
- **20** Ducks first ever team captain, Troy _____ (5)
- **21** 1999 Stanley Cup champs (6,5)

Down

- **1** Led NHL in goals, 1990 _____ Hull (5)
- **2** 1958 Vezina Winner, _____ Plante (7)
- **4** Ten-minute penalty against a player (10,7)
- **7** 1979 NHL MVP, NYI, Bryan _____ (8)
- **8** Mr. Hockey (6,4)
- **9** Jonathan Toews nickname (7,7)
- **11** Led NHL in goals 2011 ANA (5,5)
- **15** Led NHL in goals 2020, Ovechkin and (8)
- **17** Playing area in hockey (4)
- **18** Bruins mascot is a (4)
- **19** Longtime Coyotes captain, Shane _____ (4)

Puzzle #2

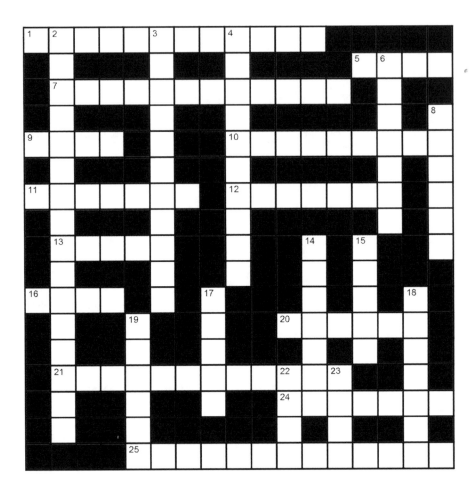

Across

1. Chicago arena (6,6)
5. 1963 NHL MVP, DET, Gordie ___ (4)
7. The Great One (5,7)
9. Hockey movie (4)
10. Ducks mascot name (4,5)
11. Led NHL in goals 1997, Keith ___ (7)
12. New Jersey Devils mascot (1,1,5)
13. 1982 Vezina winner, Billy ___ (5)
16. Retired #18 Sabres, Danny ___ (4)
20. Won back to back Lady Byng awards, Ducks, Paul ___ (6)
21. 2009 Conn Smythe PIT (6,6)
24. 2021 James Norris winner NYR (4,3)
25. 2009 Presidents' Trophy (3,4,6)

Down

2. Won 4 straight Stanley Cups in the 1980s (3,4,9)
3. 2016 James Norris winner, Kings (4,7)
4. Scored 5 goals in a game, Flames 1989 Joe ___ (10)
6. Blues captain since 2020, Ryan ___ (7)
8. Flames captain 2003-2013 Jarome ___ (6)
14. 2021 NHL MVP, Connor ___ (7)
15. St. Luis Blues mascot (5)
17. 1978 Jack Adams winner, DET Bobby ___ (5)
18. 1st Ducks coach to have a winning record during his time with the team, Mike ___ (7)
19. Actor who was a hockey player, Keanu ___ (6)
22. Oilers C, Evander ___ (4)
23. 1st Blue Jackets player to lead league in goals, Rick ___ (4)

Puzzle #3

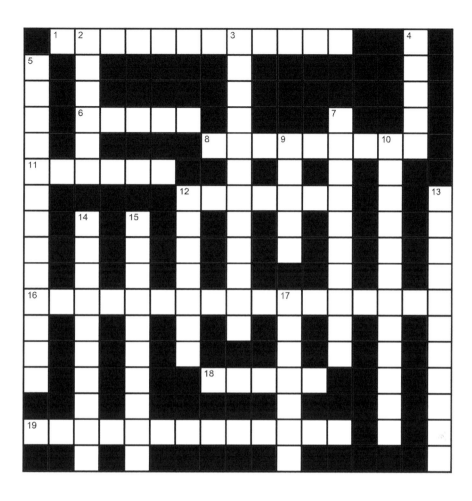

Across

1. Mr. Zero Bruins goalie (5,7)
6. 1954 James Norris winner, Red ___ (5)
8. 2020 NHL MVP, Leon ___ (9)
11. Penguins D, Kris ___ (6)
12. 1996 James Norris winner, Chris ___ (7)
16. Won Stanley Cup every year from 1956 - 1960 (8,9)
18. Stars mascot name, Victor E. ___ (5)
19. 2012 Conn Smythe LA (8,5)

Down

2. Maurice Richard nickname (6)
3. Player checks an opponent who is not in possession of the puck (12)
4. Hurricanes captain since 2019, Jordan ___ (5)
5. Holder of single season shooting percentage record (7,6)
7. TOR captain 1997-2008 (4,6)
9. A shot across the center red line and past the opposing team's goal line (5)
10. The Finnish Flash (5,7)
12. Flames moved from ATL to (7)
13. 1978 James Norris winner, NYI (5,6)
14. Bruins made the playoffs an NHL record ___ seasons in a row (6,4)
15. Sabres mascot (10)
17. Devils mascot (2,5)

Puzzle #4

Across

3. 1939 Vezina winner, Frank _____ (7)
5. 2019 Jack Adams winner, Barry _____ (5)
7. Puck material (10,6)
10. Anaheim arena (5,6)
12. Lightning (5,3)
14. Led NHL in goals 1977, Steve _____ (5)
15. Seattle (6)
18. Canucks mascot animal (5)
19. 1952 and 1953 NHL MVP DET (6,4)
20. 1948 Vezina winner, Turk _____ (5)
21. Intermission is how many minutes? (8)
22. Sharks (3,4)

Down

1. The Hammer (4,7)
2. Anaheim Ducks mascot (4,4)
3. Chicago (10)
4. 1926 NHL MVP, MTL, Nels _____ (7)
6. 47, 48, and 49 Stanley Cup champs (7,5,5)
8. Canucks arena (6,5)
9. Nikolai Khabibulin nickname (5,4)
11. Area between blue lines in the center of the ice (7,4)
13. Blue Jackets captain since 2021 Boone _____ (6)
16. 1999 NHL MVP, PIT, Jaromir _____ (4)
17. 2010 James Norris winner, Duncan _____ (5)

Puzzle #5

Across

1 Begins every game (7)
5 Hurricanes, D, Jaccob _____ (6)
8 Nashville (9)
9 2007 NHL MVP PIT (6,6)
11 Goalie, Sergei _____ (9)
12 2020 and 2021 Stanley Cup champs (5,3,9)
18 1930 NHL MVP, MTL Nels _____ (7)
19 2015 Conn Smythe winner (6,5)
20 1974 Jack Adams winner, PHI Fred _____ (5)
21 Ben Bishop nickname (3,3)
22 Most goals in a season COL, Michel _____ (6)

Down

1 2002 Jack Adams winner, PHO Bob _____ (7)
2 Celebration after a goal (5)
3 Another form of hockey (5)
4 Hurricanes original team name (7)
6 Led NHL in goals 2022 (6,8)
7 Wild mascot name (5)
8 2013 James Norris winner, MTL (2,6)
10 1974 Vezina winner PHI (6,6)
12 Rangers captain since 2022, Jacob _____ (6)
13 1989 Conn Smythe, Flames, Al ___ (8)
14 2003 Jack Adams winner, MIN Jacques _____ (7)
15 Nashville Predators mascot (5)
16 Flames player with single season record for most penalty minutes, Tim _____ (6)
17 2004 NHL MVP, Martin, TB (2,5)

Puzzle #6

Across

1. Period of time a line of players is on the ice (5)
4. Nordiques (6)
8. 2019 Conn Smythe winner (4,7)
9. Goal by team playing with less players due to penalties (11,4)
10. 1960 NHL MVP, DET Gordie ____ (4)
11. Led NHL in goals 2010 Stamkos and ____ (6)
14. 1961 NHL MVP, MTL, Bernie ____ (9)
17. 1997 and 1998 NHL MVP, Dominik BUF (5)
18. Winnipeg Jets mascot (4,1.5)
21. 2004 James Norris winner, Scott ____ (11)
22. Hard rubber disc used in hockey (4)

Down

1. 2010 NHL MVP, Henrik ____ (5)
2. Vancouver Canucks mascot (3,3,5)
3. 2009 James Norris winner, Zdeno ____ (5)
5. Nashville arena (11,5)
6. 1989 Presidents' Trophy (7,6)
7. 1989 NHL MVP LAK, Wayne ____ (7)
11. Former coach and broadcaster, Don ____ (6)
12. Artemi Panarin nickname (5,3)
13. Players who play in front of the goaltender (10)
15. Penalty called when player strikes an opponent with his elbow (8)
16. Led NHL in goals 2003, COL Milan ____ (6)
19. Dallas (5)
20. Led NHL in goals 1994 Pavel ____ (4)

Puzzle #7

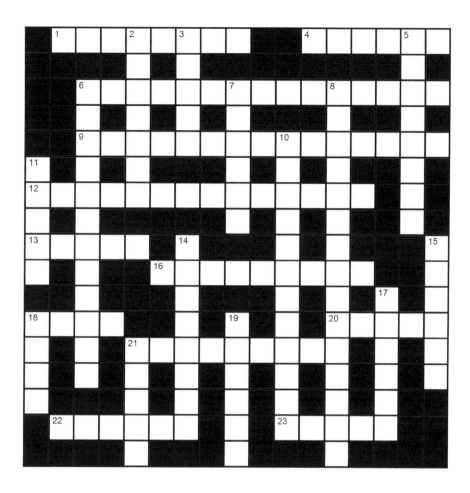

Across

1. 1938 Vezina winner, Tiny _____ (8)
4. 2016 Vezina winner, Braden _____ (6)
6. Vezina winner 2021 (4-5,6)
9. 2002 Conn Smythe DET (7,8)
12. Flames mascot name (6,3,5)
13. Flames goalie who had 3 assists in 1 game, Jeff (5)
16. Capitals mascot animal (4,5)
18. 1963 Vezina winner, Glenn _____ (4)
20. Lost Stanley Cup to TB IN 2020 (5)
21. 2012 Jack Adams winner, STL Ken _____ (9)
22. 1943 Vezina winner, Johnny _____ (6)
23. Golden Knights (5)

Down

2. Hockey movie about 1980 Olympics (7)
3. Coyotes career leaders in short handed goals, Doug _____ (5)
5. FL C, Aleksander _____ (6,2)
6. Two-minute penalty (5,7)
7. Company that founded the Ducks in 1993 (6)
8. 2014 Stanley Cup champs (3,7,5)
10. The Professor, DET (4,8)
11. 1933 NHL MVP, BOS Eddie _____ (5)
14. Washington (8)
15. Sid the Kid (6)
17. Buffalo (6)
18. Led NHL in goals 1992, Brett _____ (4)
19. 1935 Vezina winner, Lorne _____ (6)
21. 2001 Vezina winner, Dominik _____ (5)

Puzzle #8

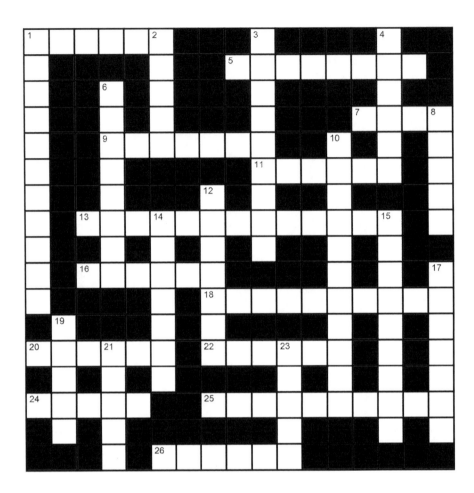

Across

1 Boston (6)
5 PIT LW, Jake ____ (8)
7 Forward who lines up near the middle of the rink, and to either side of the center (4)
9 Stanley C. ____ (7)
11 1988 Jack Adams winner, DET Jacques ____ (6)
13 Detroit arena (6,7)
16 Canucks captain since 2019, Bo____ (6)
18 Scored 5 goals in a game in 1986, Dave ____ (10)
20 Led NHL in goals 1957, ____ Howe (6)
22 1997 James Norris winner, Brian ____ (6)
24 1976 Conn Smythe, PHI Reggie ____ (5)
25 Most points by an American born player in a season, 1993 Pat ____ (10)
26 1928 NHL MVP, MTL Howie ____ (6)

Down

1 Columbus (4,7)
2 Last name of twins on Canucks (5)
3 FL C, Jonathan ____ (9)
4 New Jersey (6)
6 Led NHL in goals 1970 - 1975, Phil ____ (8)
8 Field hockey is played on ____ (5)
10 Free shot at goal (7,4)
12 1987 Conn Smythe, PHI Ron ____ (7)
14 TOR captain since 2019, John ____ (7)
15 San Jose Sharks mascot (1,1,7)
17 2010 rookie of the year, CAR, Jeff ____ (7)
19 1961 Vezina winner, Johnny ____ (5)
21 Anaheim (5)
23 2016 Jack Adams winner, Barry ____ (5)

Puzzle #9

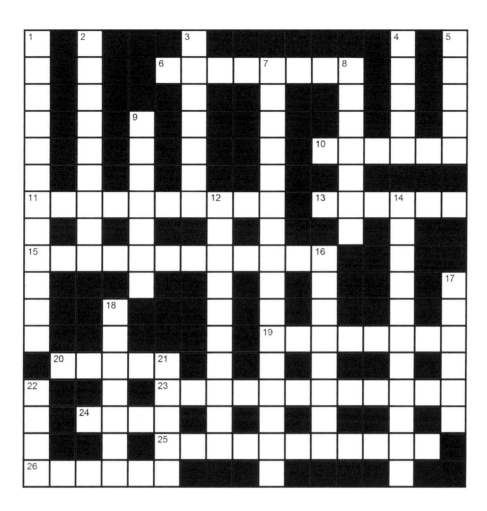

Across

6 1936 Vezina winner, Tiny ____ (8)
10 San Jose (6)
11 Type of scheduling in hockey (5,5)
13 1995 James Norris winner, Paul ____ (6)
15 2011 Stanley Cup champs (6,6)
19 Hurricanes (8)
20 Lost 2003 Stanley Cup to NJ (5)
23 First female NHL player (5,7)
24 Predators D, Roman ____ (4)
25 Diameter of puck (5,6)
26 1992 James Norris winner, Brian ____ (6)

Down

1 New York Rangers mascot (6,6)
2 Quebec (9)
3 Blackhawks (7)
4 COL D, Cale ____ (5)
5 Lost Stanley Cup to NJ in 2000 (5)
7 New Jersey Devils arena (10,6)
8 1924 NHL MVP, Ottawa, Frank ____ (7)
9 Curse of ____ (7)
12 High-scoring game (10)
14 Length of overtime period (4,7)
16 Wild captain since 2020, Jared ____ (8)
17 Lost 2004 Stanley Cup to TB (6)
18 There was no NHL season in 2005 due to a (7)
21 1937 Vezina winner, Normie ____ (5)
22 Led NHL in goals 1991, Brett ____ (4)

Puzzle #10

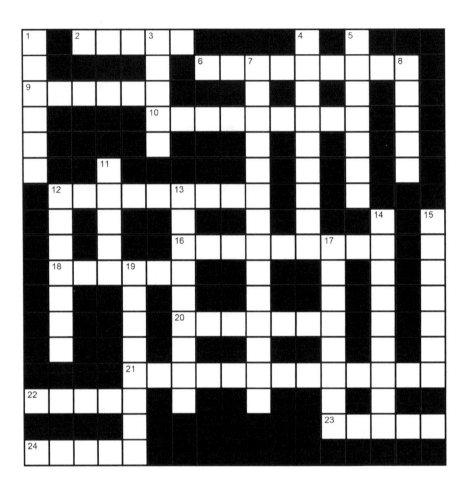

Across

2 Led NHL in goals 1962, ____ Hull (5)
6 Lost Stanley Cup to PIT in 2017 (9)
9 2001 Jack Adams winner, PHI Bill _____ (6)
10 2022 James Norris winner COL (4,5)
12 Retired #11 Sabres, Gilbert _____ (9)
16 Wild (9)
18 Lost Stanley Cup to MTL in 1986 (6)
20 1954 NHL MVP, CHI, Al ____ (7)
21 Oilers captain since 2016 (6,7)
22 1999 Vezina winner, Dominik ____ (5)
23 Predators G, Jusse _____ (5)
24 1982 Conne Smyth NYI, Mike ___ (5)

Down

1 Founded along with Canucks in 1970 (6)
3 1925 NHL MVP, Billy ____ (5)
4 Only coach suspended during Cup final (4,5)
5 1994 James Norris winner, Ray ____ (7)
7 1984 and 1985 Stanley Cup champs (8,6)
8 1996 Conn Smythe COL, Joe ___ (5)
11 1941 Vezina winner, Turk ____ (5)
12 1975 Jack Adams winner, LAK Bob ____ (7)
13 TOR captain 1957-1969 George ____ (9)
14 Canucks (9)
15 1947 NHL MVP, MTL, Maurice ____ (7)
17 Player enters the attacking zone ahead of the puck (8)
19 Gordie Howe nickname (2,6)

Puzzle #11

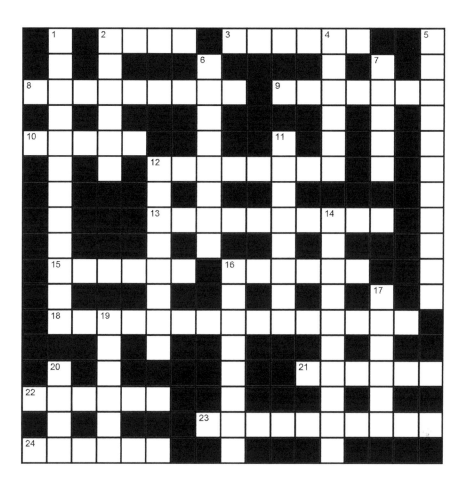

Across

2 Led NHL in goals 1951 - 1953, Gordie ____ (4)
3 Hurricanes mascot name (6)
8 Big Ben, goalie (3,6)
9 1994 NHL MVP, DET, Sergei ____ (7)
10 2011 NHL MVP, Corey ____, Ducks (5)
12 Avalanche (8)
13 Bench where players go to serve their penalty (7,3)
15 ____ Ducks (6)
16 Stars single season assist record, Neal ____ (6)
18 2006 - 2008 James Norris winner, DET (7,8)
21 2009 Jack Adams winner, BOS Claude ____ (6)
22 1984 Jack Adams winner, WAS Bryan ____ (6)
23 Capitals (10)
24 Philadelphia (6)

Down

1 Longest tenured captain NHL history 1986-2006 (5,7)
2 Ducks 1st pick in 1993 expansion draft, Guy ____ (6)
4 Stars leader in points, goals, and assists Mike ____ (6)
5 Scored first goal in NHL (4,7)
6 Red stripe at each end of the rink (4,4)
7 2015 NHL MVP, Carey ____ (5)
11 Hurricanes original location (8)
12 Ovechkin team (8)
14 2017 James Norris winner, San Jose (5,5)
16 1964 NHL MVP, Jean, MTL (8)
17 1934 NHL MVP, MTL Aurele ____ (6)
19 1975 and 1976 NHL MVP, PHI, Bobby ____ (6)
20 Led NHL in goals 1966-1969, Bobby ____ (4)

Puzzle #12

Across

4 Led NHL in goals 2004, ATL Ilya ___ (9)
8 Blackhawks captain since 2008 (8,5)
9 1998 Jack Adams winner, BOS Pat _____ (5)
10 Billy Smith nickname (7,3)
11 MTL captain 1999-2009, Saku _____ (5)
13 1948 NHL MVP, NYR, Buddy _____ (7)
16 2019 James Norris winner, Flames (4,8)
18 The red stripe that extends across the ice, midway between the two goals (6,4)
19 2018 Presidents' Trophy (9,9)
20 Penalty called when a player deliberately delays the game (5,2,4)

Down

1 Led NHL in goals 1961, Bernie _____ (9)
2 Pass from a player behind the opponent's goal to a teammate in front of the goal (4,3)
3 Lost Stanley Cup to MTL in 1969 (5)
4 Los Angeles (5)
5 NHL MVP award called (4,8,6)
6 1963 James Norris winner, ___ Pilote (6)
7 Bruins captain 1985-2000 (7,7)
10 Led NHL in goals 1964 Bobby _____ (4)
12 1998 Vezina winner BUF (7,5)
14 Players on the offensive line (center and two wings) (8)
15 COL captain for 13 years, Joe (5)
16 1999 James Norris winner, Al ___ (8)
17 2002 NHL MVP, MTL, Jose ___ (8)

Puzzle #13

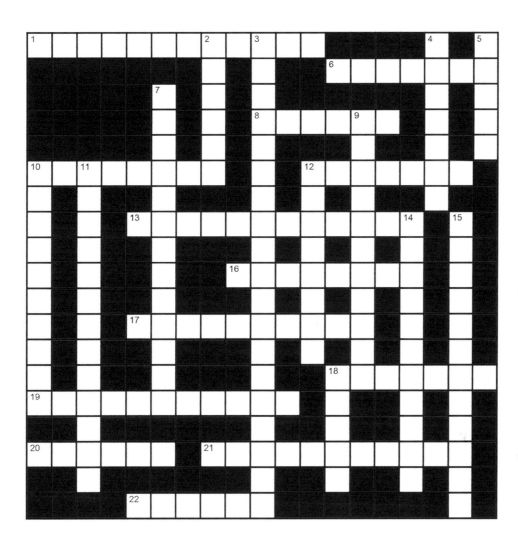

Across

1. 2007 Stanley Cup champs (7,5)
6. Hockey official (7)
8. Led NHL in goals, 1965 Norm ____ (6)
10. Eric Vail nickname (3,5)
12. Senators captain since 2021, Brady ____ (7)
13. Bruins single season record for goals and points (4,8)
16. Pass to a teammate where the puck is lifted slightly off the ice (4,4)
17. Mr. Hockey (6,4)
18. Stars captain 1994-2003, Derian ____ (7)
19. Edmonton arena (6,5)
20. 1976 James Norris winner, Denis ____ (6)
21. Wayne Gretzky nickname (3,5,3)
22. The wall surrounding the rink that keeps the puck in play (6)

Down

2. 1950 Vezina winner, Bill ____ (6)
3. Founded in 2000 (8,4,7)
4. 2008 Vezina winner, Martin ____ (7)
5. 1st Ducks player to win Hart Memorial trophy, Corey ____ (5)
7. 2010 Conn Smythe CHI (8,5)
9. Tampa arena (6,5)
10. 2021 Jack Adams winner, Rod ____ (10)
11. Vegas (6,7)
12. 1933 Vezina winner, Tiny ____ (8)
14. Term for player blocking another player (11)
15. 50 goals in 50 games (5,7)
18. Sabres goalie with most shutouts in a season, Dominik ____ (5)

Puzzle #14

Across

1. Capitals mascot name (8)
5. 2006 Conn Smythe CAR (3,4)
10. Getting the puck away from the area near your own goal (8)
11. New York (7)
13. Philadelphia Flyers' mascot (6)
15. Given to MVP (4,6)
16. Lost Stanley Cup to LAK in 2012 (6)
17. 1968 - 1975 James Norris winner BOS (5,3)
19. 2007 Presidents' Trophy (7,6)
20. Montreal arena (4,6)
21. Bruins, Stars, Tyler ___ (6)
22. 1970 rookie of the year, Gilbert ___ (9)

Down

2. Another term for hair (7)
3. Led NHL in goals 1942, Lynn ___ (7)
4. Teemu Selänne's nickname (3,7,5)
5. Lost Stanley Cup to NYI in 1982 (7)
6. 1988 Conn Smythe EDM (5,7)
7. 1978 Conn Smythe MTL, Larry ___ (8)
8. 2008 and 2009 NHL MVP, WAS (4,8)
9. 1966 Conn Smythe, DET Roger ___ (7)
10. 2021 Presidents' Trophy (8,9)
12. 2007 Vezina winner, Martin ___ (7)
14. 1973 NHL MVP, PHI, Bobby ___ (6)
17. Colorado Avalanche mascot (6)
18. Red Wings fans throw this animal on the ice (7)

Puzzle #15

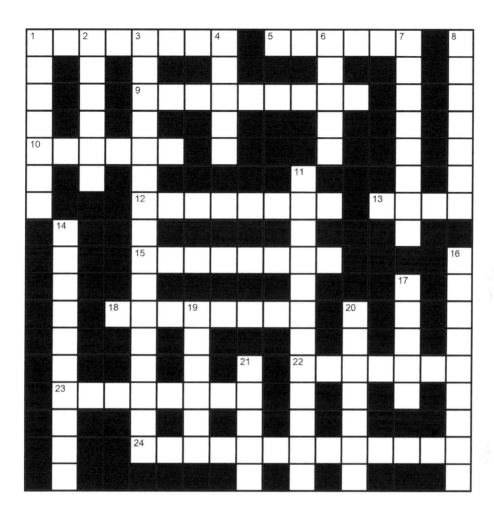

Across

1 Player rubs the palm of glove in an opponent's face (4,4)
5 Lost Stanley Cup to DAL in 1999 (6)
9 2012 Vezina winner, Henrik _____ (9)
10 4x8 area in front of goal in which opposing players may not stand unless they have the puck (6)
12 1942 NHL MVP, Tommy _____ (8)
13 Led NHL in goals 1963. Gordie
15 1927 NHL MVP, MTL Herb _____ (8)
18 Penguins mascot (8)
22 Founded along with Sabres in 1970 (7)
23 Side of stick allowed to use (4,4)
24 Pavel Bure nickname (7,6)

Down

1 Hurricanes captain for 12 years, Ron _____ (7)
2 1943 NHL MVP, BOS, Bill _____ (6)
4 1964 Vezina winner, Charlie _____ (5)
6 Led NHL in goals, 1981 Mike _____ (5)
7 Paul Newman hockey movie (4,4)
8 Kraken (7)
11 Offensive player checks an opponent in his own end (12)
14 1985 James Norris winner, EDM (4,6)
16 Oilers F, Leon _____ (9)
17 Led NHL in goals 1976, Reggie _____ (5)
20 1995 NHL MVP, PHI, Eric _____ (7)
21 1st Blue Jackets goalie with 2,000 saves in a season, Marc _____ (5)

Puzzle #16

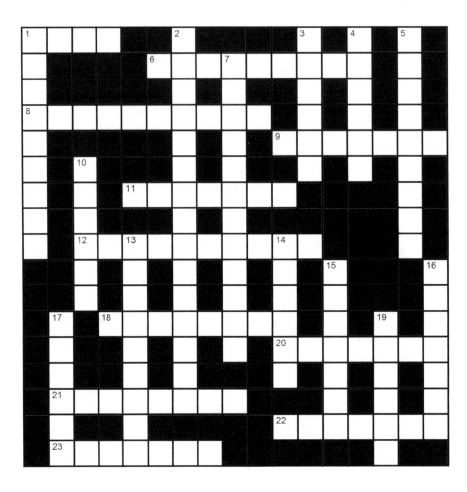

Across

1. Three forwards on the ice (center and two wings) (4)
6. The neutral area between the two blue lines (6,3)
8. 1960 James Norris winner, MTL (4,6)
9. 1988 James Norris winner, Ray ____ (7)
11. Ducks single season assist record, Ryan ____ (7)
12. Toronto (5,5)
18. 1956 NHL MVP, Jean ____ (8)
20. 1990 Conn Smythe EDM, Bill ____ (7)
21. 2012 James Norris winner, Erik ____ (8)
22. Led NHL in goals 1960, Bronco ____ (7)
23. Rangers (3,4)

Down

1. COL captain since 2012, Gabriel ____ (9)
2. 2008 Stanley Cup champs (7,3,5)
3. tallest goalie in NHL history, Ben ____ (6)
4. 1987 Jack Adams winner, DET Jacques ____ (6)
5. 1st Flames goalie with 10 shutouts in a season, Miikka ____ (9)
7. Bobby Hull nickname (3,6,3)
10. 2009 Vezina winner, Tim ____ (6)
13. When a team has a one or two man advantage because of penalties (5,4)
14. Marc-Andre ____, goalie (6)
15. 2000 NHL MVP, STL, Chris ____ (7)
16. 1990 Jack Adams winner, Jets Bob ____ (7)
17. DET captain since 2020, Dylan ____ (6)
19. 1996 Jack Adams winner, DET Scotty ____ (6)

Puzzle #17

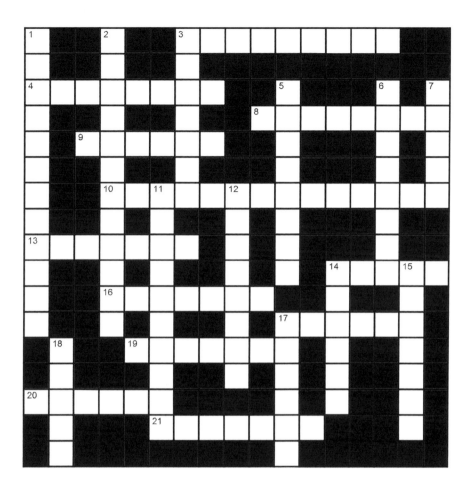

Across

3 Jets C, Mark _____ (9)
4 Lost Stanley Cup to DET in 1998 (8)
8 Canadiens (8)
9 Georges _____ (6)
10 Team owned by Wayne Gretsky (7,7)
13 2020 Jack Adams winner, Bruce _____ (7)
14 Led NHL in goals 1979 Mike _____ (5)
16 Flames LW, Matthew _____ (7)
17 Avalanche mascot name _____ the St. Bernard (6)
19 2000 James Norris winner, Chris _____ (7)
20 Lost Stanley Cup to PHI in 1975 (6)
21 Penalty called when a player uses the blade of his stick to grab opponent from behind (7)

Down

1 Henri Richard nickname (6,6)
2 First player to score 100 pointt in single season (4,8)
3 Led NHL in goals, 1999 Teemu _____ (7)
5 Another name for the net or goal (4,4)
6 Ottawa (8)
7 Lost Stanley Cup to MTL in 1968 (5)
11 Number of offensive players heading into the attacking zone is greater than the number of defenders (3,3,4)
12 Pittsburgh Penguins mascot (8)
14 NYI C, Mathew _____ (6)
15 Hockey jersey (7)
17 1970 Stanley Cup champs (6)
18 Zdeno _____ (5)

Puzzle #18

Across

1. Led NHL in goals 1947, ____ Richard (7)
3. 1983 Jack Adams winner, CHI Orval ____ (7)
8. Lost Stanley Cup to PIT in 1991 (9)
11. 2012 Stanley Cup champs (3,7,5)
13. 1927 - 1929 Vezina winner, George ____ (10)
15. 1994 Jack Adams winner, Jacques NYJ (7)
16. TB D, Victor ____ (6)
18. Red Wings original team name (7)
19. Team with 1st ever NHL mascot (6)
20. 1973 Vezina winner, Ken ____ (6)
21. Lost Stanley Cup to BOS in 2011 (7)
22. Led NHL in goals 1959, Jean ____ (8)

Down

1. Player that beat a fan with a shoe in 1979 (4,7)
2. Denver arena (4,5)
3. Senators LW, Brady ____ (7)
4. Coyotes goalie who scored a goal in 2013, Mike ____ (5)
5. Led NHL in goals 1958, Dickie ____ (5)
6. 1997 Conn Smythe DET, Mike ___ (6)
7. 2011 James Norris winner, Nicklas ____ (8)
9. Predators (9)
10. Youngest Flames player to score 100 goals, Sean ____ (7)
12. Devils (3,6)
14. Check where a player sticks out his hip (3,5)
17. Flames original city (7)

Puzzle #19

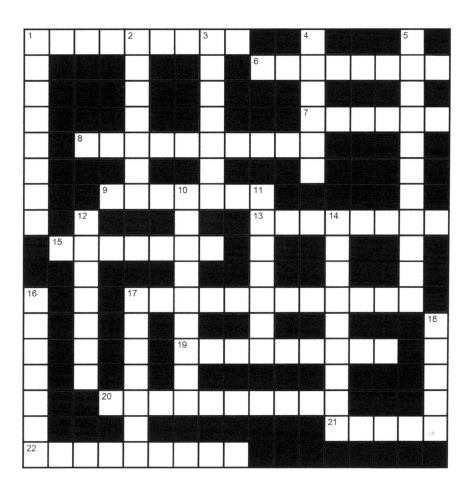

Across

1. Poke with stick at the puck to dislodge it and take it away (4,5)
6. Flames LW, Johnny _____ (8)
7. 1967 James Norris winner, Harry _____ (6)
8. 1990 James Norris winner, Bruins (3,7)
9. 1983 Vezina winner, Pete ___ (7)
13. Teeth (8)
15. Oilers and Rangers, 6x Cup champ, Mark _____ (7)
17. 2004 Conn Smythe TB (4,8)
19. Last player to play without helmet, Craig _____ (9)
20. Senators captain 1999-2013, Daniel _____ (10)
21. 1938 NHL MVP BOS, Eddie _____ (5)
22. Blackhawks mascot (5,4)

Down

1. Pittsburgh (8)
2. 1981 James Norris winner, Randy _____ (7)
3. Sharks captain since 2019, Logan _____ (7)
4. NJ C, Jack _____ (6)
5. 1999 Presidents' Trophy (6,5)
10. Dave Schultz nickname (3,6)
11. 1951 NHL MVP, BOS, Milt _____ (7)
12. Penguins, Mario ____ (7)
14. Montreal (9)
16. Led NHL in goals 1946, Gaye _____ (7)
17. 1946 NHL MVP, CHI, Max _____ (7)
18. Vegas captain since 2020, Mark _____ (5)

Puzzle #20

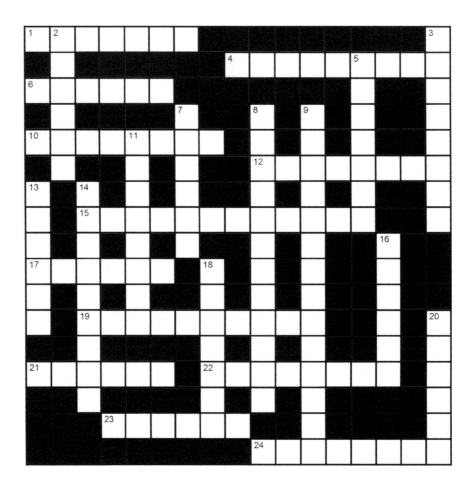

Across

1 Referees in hockey (7)
4 Lost Stanley Cup to NYI in 1981 (9)
6 1975 Conn Smythe PHI, Bernie ____ (6)
10 2003 NHL MVP, Peter ____ (8)
12 Led NHL in goals 2015 (8)
15 Patrick Roy nickname (5,7)
17 1989 Stanley Cup champs (6)
19 1955 - 1958 James Norris winner, MTL (4,6)
21 1949 Vezina winner, Bill ____ (6)
22 2016 and 2017 Stanley Cup champs (8)
23 1976 Jack Adams winner, BOS Don ____ (6)
24 Devils captain since 2020, Nico ____ (8)

Down

2 Bruins D, Charlie ____ (6)
3 1934 Vezina winner, Charlie ____ (8)
5 1955 Vezina winner, Terry ____ (7)
7 Flyers mascot name (6)
8 Most NHL season wins (5,7)
9 Hockey movie Ducks (3,6,5)
11 1965 Conn Smythe MTL Jean ____ (8)
13 1986 James Norris winner, Paul ____ (6)
14 New York (9)
16 2000 Stanley Cup champs (6)
18 Bruins captain for 14 years, Dit ____ (7)
20 1st Sabres goalie with 40 wins in a season, Ryan ____ (6)

Puzzle #21

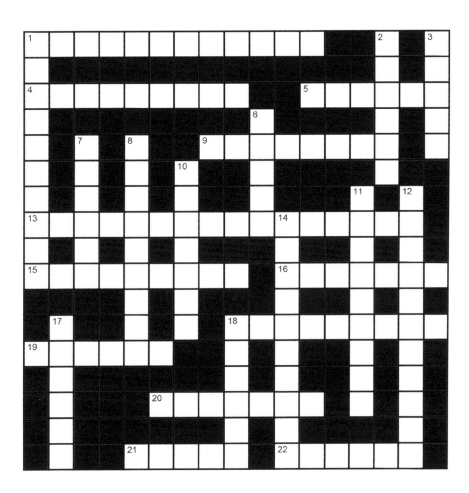

Across

1. 1952 Vezina winner, DET (5,7)
4. 2020 James Norris winner, Predators (5,4)
5. 2x Lady Byng winner, Joe _____ (6)
9. 1932 Vezina winner, Charlie _____ (8)
13. Award for most gentlemanly player (4,4,8)
15. Colorado (9)
16. Suspended eight time during his career, Ducks Chris _____ (7)
18. When a player is clear of the defense and can go towards goal unimpeded (9)
19. 1986 Jack Adams winner, EDM Glen _____ (6)
20. Kings captain since 2016, Anze _____ (7)
21. 1993 Jack Adams winner, TOR Pat _____ (5)
22. Lost Stanley Cup to PIT in 2016 (6)

Down

1. 2017 Jack Adams winner, John _____ (10)
2. Edmonton (6)
3. Lost Stanley Cup to MTL in 1993 (5)
6. 2015 Vezina winner, Carey _____ (5)
7. Led NHL in goals 1995, Peter _____ (6)
8. First player to win Kelly, Calder, and Stanley cups (3,6)
10. Lost Stanley Cup to NYR in 1994 (7)
11. 2007 Jack Adams winner, VAN Alain _____ (9)
12. Beat top seeded TB in 2019 playoffs (4,7)
14. 1967 Stanley Cup champs (5,5)
17. 1974 Conn Smythe PHI, Bernie _____ (6)
18. 1941 Stanley Cup Champs (6)

Puzzle #22

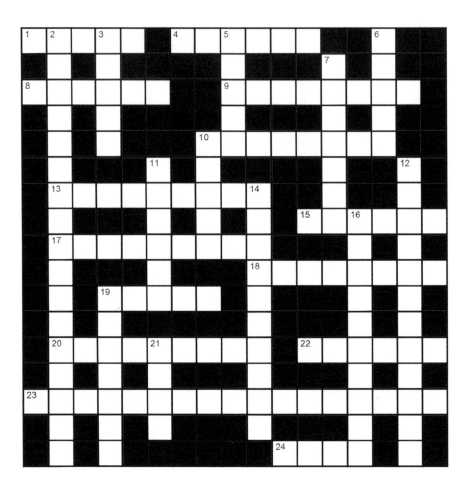

Across

1. 1983 Conn Smythe NYI, Billy ___ (5)
4. Led NHL in goals 1980 Charlie ___ (6)
8. Hurricanes mascot (6)
9. COL Mikko ___ (8)
10. Blue Jackets (8)
13. Avalanche used to be the Quebec ___ (9)
15. 1982 James Norris winner, Doug ___ (6)
17. Led NHL in goals 2000 FL (5,4)
18. 1974 NHL MVP, BOS, Phil ___ (8)
19. 1996 Vezina winner WAS, Jim ___ (5)
20. 1985 Vezina winner, Pelle ___ (9)
22. VAN D, Quinn ___ (6)
23. Led NHL in goals 2007 TB (7,10)
24. Winnipeg (4)

Down

2. Penalties given to players from each team at the same time (8,9)
3. Number of major penalties before ejection (5)
5. Led NHL in goals 1988, ___ Lemieux (5)
6. COL D, Devon ___ (5)
7. Machine used to prepare ice (7)
10. Only player in NHL history to be suspended for life, Billy ___ (5)
11. Doug Gilmour nickname (6)
12. 2000 Conn Smythe NJ (5,7)
14. Player on one knee sweeps stick across ice to take puck away from another player (5,5)
16. Kings (3,7)
19. Vancouver (7)
21. Stars, Jamie ___ (4)

Puzzle #23

Across

2 Ducks (7)
4 Stars captain since 2013 (5,4)
8 1939 NHL MVP MTL, Toe ____ (5)
10 Pinning puck against the boards causing play to stop (8,3,4)
12 Bruins captain 2006-2019 (5,5)
14 1982 Jack Adams winner, Jets Tom ____ (4)
16 1942 Vezina winner, Frank ____ (7)
18 Joe Thornton nickname (6,3)
19 St Louis (5)
20 1954 Vezina winner, Harry ____ (6)
22 Arizona Coyotes original name (4)
24 1986-2006, 668 goals, Lucky Luc (10)
25 TOR RW, Mitchell ____ (6)

Down

1 1940 NHL MVP, DET, Ebbie ____ (10)
2 2021 Conn Smythe winner (6,11)
3 1979 Jack Adams winner, NYI Al ____ (6)
5 1st emergency goalie to win a game, David ____ (5)
6 Hockey is national game of ____ (5)
7 Bruins, Patrice (8)
9 Coyotes Oliver (5,7)
11 1967 Conn Smythe TOR, Dave ____ (4)
13 Al the Octopus namesake (2,7)
15 1970, 1971, and 1972 NHL MVP, BOS (5,3)
17 1991 NHL MVP, STL, Brett ____ (4)
21 Bailey is a ____ (4)
23 Minnesota (4)

Puzzle #24

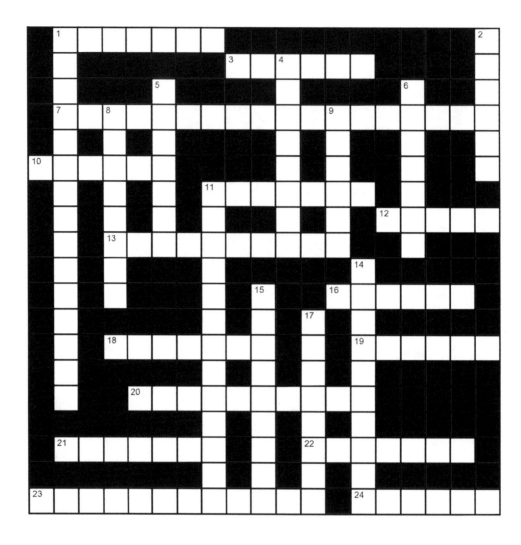

Across
1. 1987 Vezina winner, Ron ____ (7)
3. 2022 Jack Adams winner, Darryl ____ (6)
7. Rod Langway nickname, Capitals defenseman (9,2,7)
10. 1990 Stanley Cup champs (6)
11. Player who wears C on jersey (7)
12. 1989 Jack Adams winner, MTL Pat ____ (5)
13. Carolina (10)
16. 1962 NHL MVP, MTL, Jacques ____ (6)
18. 1977 and 1978 NHL MVP, MTL, Guy ____ (7)
19. Bruins single season record for most point per game, Bill ____ (6)
20. Hatchet Man, goalie Islanders (5,5)
21. 2017 NHL MVP, Connor ____ (7)
22. 1953 Vezina winner, Terry ____ (7)
23. 2018 James Norris winner, TB (6,6)
24. Blackhawks player with most points in a season, Denis ____ (6)

Down
1. Lifting the puck off the ice by flipping it with the blade of the stick (8,3,4)
2. 1931 and 1932 NHL MVP, MTL Howie ____ (6)
4. 2006 NHL MVP, Joe ____ (8)
5. 1992 NHL MVP NYR, Mark ____ (7)
6. 1993 Vezina winner, Ed ____ (7)
8. Led NHL in goals 2006, Sharks Jonathan ____ (8)
9. Lost 2001 Stanley Cup to COL (6)
11. Seattle arena (7,6)
14. 2015 Stanley Cup champs (10)
15. Flames G, Jacob ____ (9)
17. 1980 James Norris winner, Larry ____ (8)

Puzzle #25

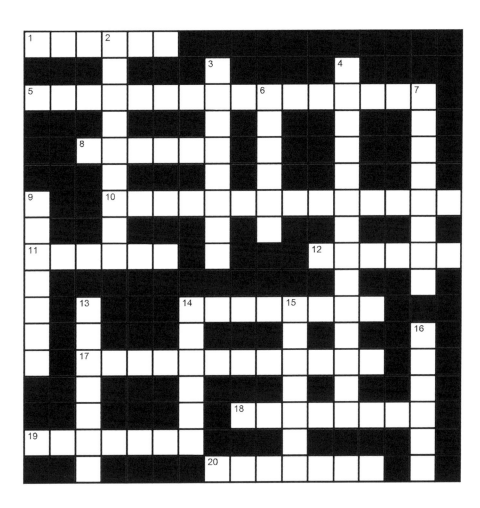

Across

1. 1977 Jack Adams winner, MTL Scotty _____ (6)
5. 2012 Presidents' Trophy (9,7)
8. 1967 and 1968 NHL MVP, CHI, Stan ___ (6)
10. 1994 Presidents' Trophy (3,4,7)
11. 1979 Conn Smythe MTL, Bob ____ (6)
12. 1975 Vezina winner, Bernie ___ (6)
14. 1959 NHL MVP, NYR, Andy _____ (8)
17. 2019 Stanley Cup champs (2,5,5)
18. Shot where player takes a big swing before hitting the puck (4,4)
19. 1993 James Norris winner, Chris _____ (7)
20. Led NHL in goals 1987, Wayne _____ (7)

Down

2. COL C, Nathan ____ (9)
3. 1923 Stanley Cup champs (8)
4. Led NHL in goals 2021 (6,8)
6. Longtime PHI captain, Bobby _____ (6)
7. Penalty where player jabs blade of his stick at opponent (8)
9. Led NHL in goals 1993 Alexander _____ (7)
13. 1990 NHL MVP, EDM, Mark ____ (7)
14. 1939 Stanley Cup champs (6)
15. 2018 Jack Adams winner, Gerard ____ (7)
16. 1991 Jack Adams winner, STL Brian _____ (6)

Puzzle #26

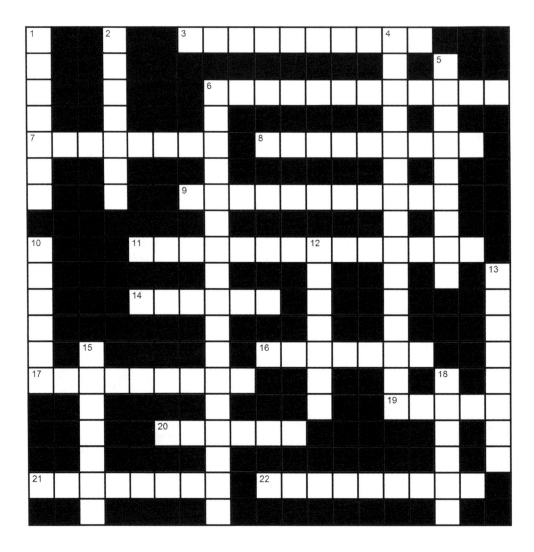

Across

3 1962, 1963, and 1964 Stanley Cup champs (5,5)
6 1974 Vezina winner, CHI (4,8)
7 2001 - 2003 James Norris winner, Nicklas ____ (8)
8 1993 Stanley Cup champs (9)
9 1998 Presidents' Trophy (6,5)
11 Penalty that has not yet resulted in a stoppage of play (7,7)
14 Kings mascot name (6)
16 1984 Conn Smythe EDM, Mark ____ (7)
17 2001 Stanley Cup champs (9)
19 4x Hart Trophy winner, Bruins Eddie ____ (5)
20 Oilers mascot name (6)
21 Highest single season save % CAR history, Anton ____ (8)
22 1973 Conn Smythe MTL, Yvan ____ (9)

Down

1 Sabres single season goals record, Alexander ____ (7)
2 1959 James Norris winner, Tom ____ (7)
4 2022 Presidents' Trophy (7,8)
5 Dallas Stars original location (9)
6 2019 Presidents' Trophy (5,3,9)
10 One of 1st players to always wear a helmet, CHI, Stan ____ (6)
12 Player that flinches away from the puck (4,3)
13 Canadiens captain 1961-1971, Jean ____ (8)
15 1977 Conn Smythe, MTL Guy ____ (7)
18 Coyotes mascot name (6)

Puzzle #27

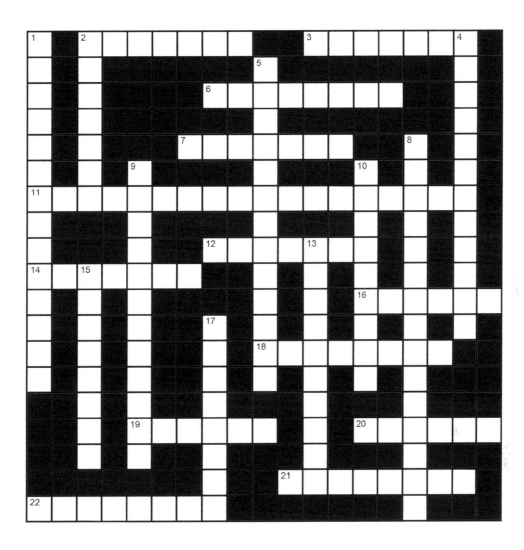

Across

2. Led NHL in goals 1955, Maurice _____ (7)
3. 1989 James Norris winner, Chris _____ (7)
6. 1930 Vezina winner, Tiny _____ (8)
7. 2004 Vezina winner, Martin _____ (7)
11. 2018 Stanley Cup champs (10,8)
12. 1st Blue Jackets player with an 80 point season, Artemi _____ (7)
14. 1996 NHL MVP, PIT, Mario _____ (7)
16. STL captain 1979-1988 Brian _____ (6)
18. 1980 Conn Smythe NYI, Bryan _____ (8)
19. 1929 Stanley Cup champs (6)
20. 1962 Vezina winner, Jacques _____ (6)
21. 1920 and 1921 Stanley Cup champs (8)
22. COL goalie with most wins in a season, Semyon _____ (8)

Down

1. 2014 Conn Smythe LA (6,8)
2. 1940 Stanley Cup champs (7)
4. 2000 Presidents' Trophy (2,5,5)
5. Lost Stanley Cup to Capitals in 2018 (6,7)
8. New York Islanders mascot (6,3,6)
9. 2017 Conn Smythe winner (6,6)
10. North Stars (9)
13. 1991 James Norris winner, BOS (3,7)
15. Gordie Howe nickname (2,6)
17. Wild, LW, Kirill _____ (8)

Puzzle #28

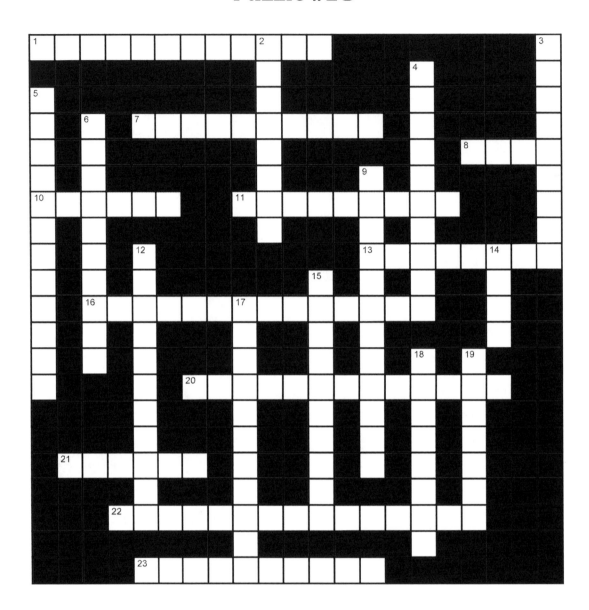

Across

1. Led NHL in goals 2016 (4,8)
7. 1961 Stanley Cup champs (10)
8. Cable sports channel (4)
10. The middle player on the forward line of a hockey team (6)
11. 1st player to score more than 50 goal in a season, 1967 CHI (5,4)
13. Post-season games (8)
16. 1927 Stanley Cup champs (6,8)
20. Actor in The Mighty Ducks (6,7)
21. Country most hockey players are from (6)
22. 2008 Presidents' Trophy (7,3,5)
23. Actor in Slap Shot (4,6)

Down

2. TB F, Nikita _____ (8)
3. 1980, 1981, 1982, and 1983 Stanley Cup champs (9)
4. 1932 Stanley Cup champs (5,5)
5. 1980 Winter Olympics (7,2,3)
6. Rob Lowe movie (10)
9. Lars-Erik Sjöberg nickname (3,9)
12. 2013 Conn Smythe CHI (7,4)
14. People who watch hockey (4)
15. 1st number retired by COL #77 (3,7)
17. Team U.S. beat in 1980 Olympics (6,5)
18. 2009 Stanley Cup champs (8)
19. Canadian hockey movie (3,4)

Puzzle #29

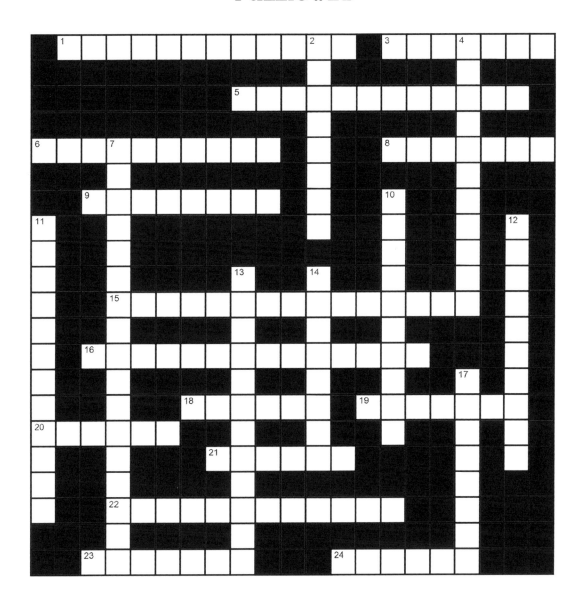

Across

1. 1985 Conn Smythe EDM (5,7)
3. 2003 Vezina winner, Martin ____ (7)
5. Penalty where player is suspended for rest of game (5,7)
6. 2010 Stanley Cup champs (10)
8. NYR LW, Artemi ____ (7)
9. The blue line dividing center ice (neutral zone) from the end zones (4,4)
15. 1997 and 1998 Stanley Cup champs (7,3,5)
16. Toronto Maple Leafs mascot (7,3,4)
18. Lost Stanley Cup to CHI in 2010 (6)
19. 1st Blackhawks goalie with 40+ wins in a season, Ed ____ (7)
20. Arizona Coyotes mascot (6)
21. Lost Stanley Cup to CHI in 2013 (6)
22. Cujo nickname, goalie (6,6)
23. 1st Blackhawk to lead league in goal and points, Doug ____ (7)
24. Edmonton Oilers mascot (6)

Down

2. Player kicks the blade of his stick as it carries the puck (4,4)
4. Relocated in 1993 (6,5)
7. 2001 Presidents' Trophy (8,9)
10. 2006 Stanley Cup champs (10)
11. Led NHL in goals 2019 (4,8)
12. First black player in NHL (6,4)
13. 2016 Conn Smythe winner (6,6)
14. 1981 Jack Adams winner, STL Red (8)
17. Bruins single season assist record (5,3)

Puzzle #30

Across
1. 1945 Stanley Cup champs (5,5)
4. 1993 NHL MVP, PIT, Mario ____ (7)
5. Led NHL in goals 2017 (6,6)
8. 2004 Jack Adams winner, TB John ____ (10)
13. Bruins goalie with most shutouts in a season, Hal ____ (7)
14. 1984 James Norris winner, Rod ____ (7)
16. Won Conn Smythe but didn't win Stanley Cup, 2003 (4,9,7)
17. Buffalo arena (7,6)
18. 2015 Jack Adams winner, Bob ____ (7)
19. Hurricanes captain on 2006 Cup winning team, Rod ____ (10)
20. 1977 James Norris winner, Larry ____ (8)
21. 2011 Presidents' Trophy (9,7)

Down
2. Oilers (8)
3. Lost Stanley Cup to DET in 1997 (6)
6. 1997 Vezina winner BUF (7,5)
7. Five-minute penalty (5,7)
9. Bruins captain since 2020 (7,8)
10. Bruins mascot (6,3,5)
11. The zone where the opponent's goal is located (9,4)
12. 1988 Presidents' Trophy (7,6)
15. Won gold medal and Stanley Cup in same year (3,6)

Puzzle #31

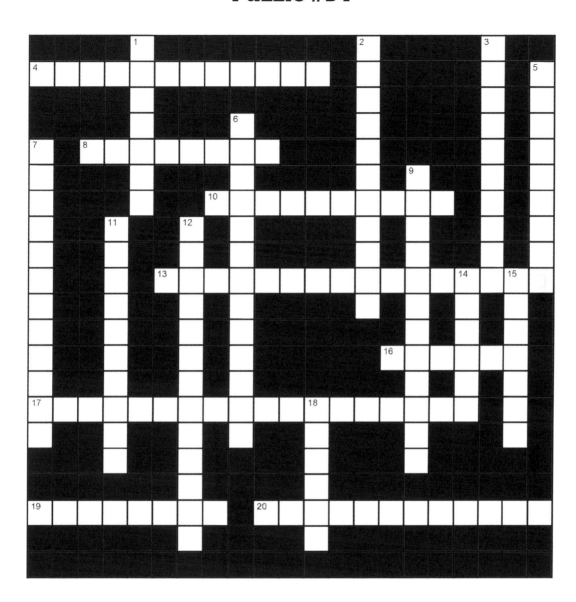

Across

4 Led NHL in goals, 1982-1985 (5,7)
8 2002 Vezina winner, Jose ___ (8)
10 1989 Vezina winner MTL (7,3)
13 2008 Conn Smythe DET (6,10)
16 1981 Conn Smythe NYI, Butch ___ (6)
17 Philadelphia Flyers nickname (5,6,7)
19 2019 NHL MVP, Nikita ___ (8)
20 Led NHL in goals 2018 (4,8)

Down

1 1988 NHL MVP, PIT, Mario ___ (7)
2 2014 James Norris winner, CHI (6,5)
3 1987 James Norris winner, BOS (3,7)
5 COL LW, Gabriel ___ (9)
6 Record for most points in single period (5,8)
7 Penguins captain since 2007 (6,6)
9 Blackhawks single season record for shutouts (4,8)
11 1942 Stanley Cup champs (5,5)
12 Led NHL in goals 2012 (6,7)
14 Lost Stanley Cup to Oilers in 1990 (6)
15 1933 Stanley Cup champs (7)
18 Los Angeles Kings mascot (6)

Puzzle #32

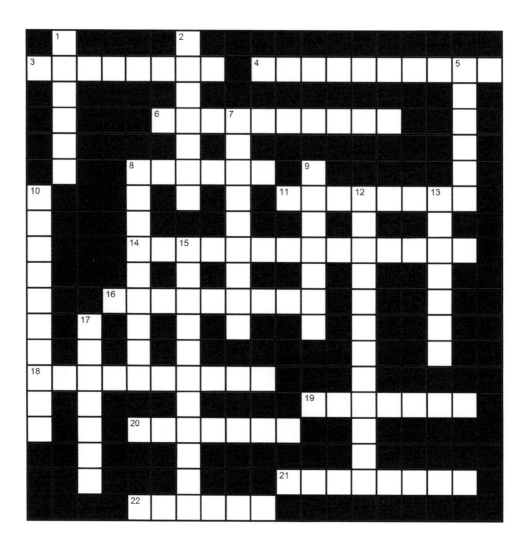

Across

3 2008 Jack Adams winner, WAS Bruce _____ (8)
4 1951 Stanley Cup champs (5,5)
6 2013 Stanley Cup champs (10)
8 Lost Stanley Cup to STL in 2019 (6)
11 Lost Stanley Cup to ANA in 2007 (8)
14 When player uses up penalty time by circling back to own goal with puck (7,3,4)
16 1996 Stanley Cup champs (9)
18 Player with lifetime suspension (5,5)
19 Bruins coach with highest winning % Tom _____ (7)
20 Rangers captain for 10 years, Mark _____ (7)
21 Jets (8)
22 Panthers captain since 2018, Aleksander _____ (6)

Down

1 Coyotes mascot name (6)
2 Led NHL in goals 1978, Guy _____ (7)
5 1974 and 1975 Stanley Cup champs (6)
7 1986 Stanley Cup champs (9)
8 2017 Vezina winner, Sergei _____ (9)
9 Led NHL in goals 1943 and 1944, Doug _____ (7)
10 TB mascot (10)
12 2018 Conn Smythe winner (4,8)
13 Led NHL in goals 1950, Maurice _____ (7)
15 Chance (mascot) is a _____ (4,7)
17 1991 Vezina winner, Ed _____ (7)

Puzzle #33

Across

1. Player pulls down an opponent with his stick or hand or by sticking out his leg (8)
3. TB G, Andrei _____ (11)
6. Led NHL in goals 1980 Blaine _____ (9)
10. 1935 and 1936 NHL MVP, BOS Eddie _____ (5)
12. Style of goaltending made popular by Patrick Roy (6)
13. 1995 Vezina winner, Dominik _____ (5)
15. Bruins player with most penalty minutes in a season, 1988, Jay _____ (6)
16. New York arena (7,6,6)
20. 2013 Jack Adams winner, Paul _____ (7)
21. Minnesota Wild mascot (5)
22. Lost Stanley Cup to BOS in 1970 (5)
23. 1985 Jack Adams winner, PHI Mike _____ (6)
24. 1999 Jack Adams winner, OTT Jacques _____ (6)

Down

1. 2011 Vezina winner, Tim _____ (6)
2. 1965 James Norris winner, Pierre _____ (6)
4. 2020 Conn Smythe winner (6,6)
5. Sabres drafted this player in 1974 who turned out to not even exist, Tokyo _____ (7)
6. 2007 Conn Smythe ANA (5,11)
7. 2015 Presidents' Trophy (3,4,7)
8. Led NHL in goals 2010 Crosby and (7)
9. NHL MVP every year from 1980-1987 (5,7)
11. 1951 Vezina winner, Al _____ (7)
14. Bernie Geoffrion nickname (4,4)
15. 1st player with # retired by Flames #9 Lanny _____ (8)
17. 1980 Jack Adams winner, PHI Pat _____ (5)
18. Vegas C, Jack _____ (6)
19. 2012 NHL MVP, Evgeni _____ (6)

Puzzle #34

Across

1. Three goals scored by a player in one game (3,5)
7. 1949 NHL MVP, DET Sid _____ (4)
8. Avalanche original city (6)
9. 2010 Jack Adams winner, PHO Dave _____ (7)
11. Senators (6)
12. 1957 and 1958 NHL MVP DET (6,4)
13. Toronto arena (10,5)
16. Most points and goals ever by an american player, Stars (4,6)
17. TB C, Brayden _____ (5)
18. Stars (6)
20. Led NHL in goals, 1998 _____ Selanne (5)
21. 1983 James Norris winner, WASH (3,7)
22. Bruins F, David _____ (8)

Down

2. 2013 NHL MVP WAS (4,8)
3. Number of seasons played by Gretsky (6)
4. 2013 Presidents' Trophy (7,10)
5. Predators captain since 2017, Roman _____ (4)
6. 2016 NHL MVP, Patrick _____ (4)
8. 1992 Jack Adams winner, VAN Pat _____ (5)
9. Maple Leafs (7)
10. 1964 James Norris winner, CHI (6,6)
14. 2011 Conn Smythe BOS (3,6)
15. Wore number zero (4,6)
16. 2010 Vezina winner, Ryan _____ (6)
19. Blues mascot (5)

Puzzle #35

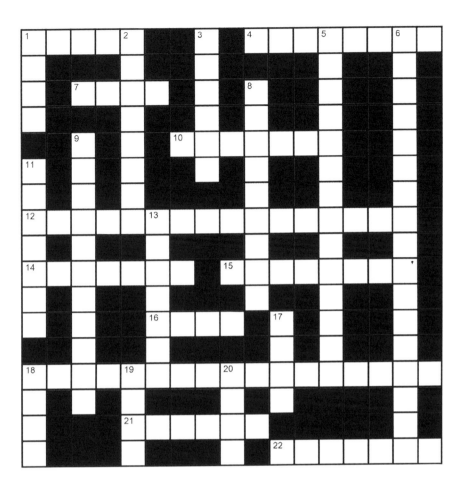

Across
1. 2001 NHL MVP, COL, Joe _____ (5)
4. 1st player to have jersey retired by the Bruins, Lioniel #3 (8)
7. Body part not allowed to hit (4)
10. 1937 NHL MVP, MTL Babe _____ (7)
12. Winnipeg arena (6,4,6)
14. 1st Blue Jackets captain, Lyle _____ (7)
15. 1984 Vezina winner, Tom _____ (8)
16. 1st black player in the NHL, Willie _____ (4)
18. 2022 Stanley Cup champs (8,9)
21. Calgary (6)
22. Devils captain 1992-2004, Scott _____ (7)

Down
1. Goalie blocks shot (4)
2. 1995 Jack Adams winner, Quebec Marc _____ (8)
3. 2000 Vezina winner, Olaf _____ (6)
5. Washington arena (6,3,5)
6. Capitals captain since 2009 (9,8)
8. NYR C, Mika _____ (9)
9. 2000 Jack Adams winner, STL Joel _____ (11)
11. Referee drops the puck between two opposing players to start or resume the game after a stoppage in play (4,3)
13. Coyotes (7)
17. Led NHL in goals 1956, _____ Beliveau (4)
18. Rangers captain 1926-1937, Bill _____ (4)
19. 2006 Jack Adams winner, BUF Lindy _____ (4)
20. Led NHL in goals 1949 Sid _____ (4)

Puzzle #36

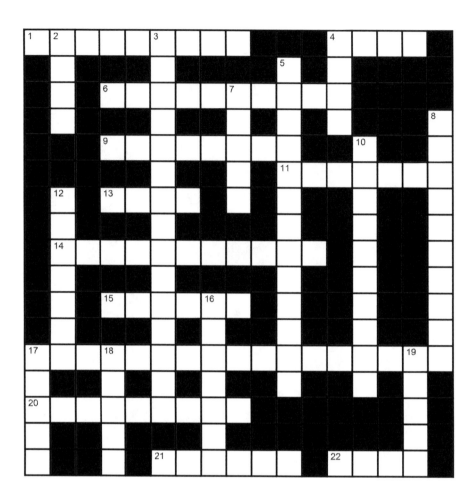

Across
1 San Jose arena (3,6)
4 Amount of time Conn Smythe winner was not on Stanley Cup winning team (4)
6 Penguins (10)
9 Pass where player with puck speeding toward goal suddenly leaves it motionless for a trailing teammate (4,4)
11 Position behind the center (7)
13 Gordie ____, Red Wings (4)
14 Played in summer Olympics (5,6)
15 Vega Golden Knights mascot (6)
17 Won 4 straight Stanley Cups in the 1970s (8,9)
20 Senators mascot (9)
21 1976 Vezina winner, Ken ____ (6)
22 Jarome Iginla nickname (4)

Down
2 Led NHL in goals 2014 ____ Ovechkin (4)
3 Columbus arena (10,5)
4 1988 Vezina winner, Grant ____ (4)
5 Player drives the shaft of his stick into an opponent while holding on to the stick with both hands (5,8)
7 1998 James Norris winner, Rob ____ (5)
8 Stars original team name (5,5)
10 DET captain 1962-1973, Alex ____ (10)
12 Sabres (7)
16 Flames (7)
17 1st Blue Jacket to win ROY, Steve ____ (5)
18 1st Stars goalie with 40 wins in a season, Marty ____ (5)
19 Edouard Cyrille Lalonde nickname (5)

Puzzle #37

Across

1. 2018 NHL MVP, Taylor ____ (4)
5. Teemu Selänne number (5)
7. A major penalty called when a player hits his opponent with the butt end of the shaft of his hocke (4,6)
10. 2003 Stanley Cup champs (3,6,6)
11. Won NHL ROY at age 31, Sergei ____ (7)
12. 1950 NHL MVP, NYR, Chuck ____ (6)
13. Shot made by snapping wrists as puck hits the blade of the stick (5,4)
14. Blades is a ____ (4)
18. Stars mascot is an (5)
19. Sabres mascot name (10)
21. Blue Jackets, Patrik ____ (5)
22. 1997 Jack Adams winner BUF Ted ____ (5)
23. 2006 Vezina winner, Miikka ____ (9)
24. CHI RW, Patrick ____ (4)
25. 1969 NHL MVP, BOS, PHI (8)

Down

2. Vezina winner 2019, TB (6,11)
3. Led NHL in goals 1948, Ted ____ (7)
4. Vezina winner 1944 - 1947 MTL (4,6)
6. 1962 James Norris winner, Doug ____ (6)
7. 2011 Jack Adams winner, PIT Dan ____ (6)
8. Kent Nilsson nickname (3,5,3)
9. Tempe arena (6,5)
15. 1941 NHL MVP, BOS, Bill ____ (6)
16. MTL mascot (6)
17. Blues (2,5)
19. penalty box (3,3)
20. Original Winnipeg Jets mascot (5)

Puzzle #38

Across

1. The player who guards the goal (6)
3. Predators mascot name (5)
5. 1961 James Norris winner, ___ Harvey (4)
7. 1986 Vezina winner, John ___ (13)
12. Number of teams that never won Stanley Cup (6)
13. 2014 NHL MVP PIT (6,6)
14. Bruins LW, Brad ___ (8)
16. 1940 Vezina winner, David ___ (4)
19. A deceptive move or fake used to get around an opponent (4)
21. Detroit Red Wings mascot (2,3,7)
22. Led NHL in goals 1980 Danny ___ (4)
23. Vezina winner 2018, Pekka ___ (5)
24. 1979 James Norris winner, Denis ___ (6)
25. 2015 James Norris winner, Erik ___ (8)
26. Red Wings (7)

Down

1. A penalty resulting in the player being suspended for the remainder of the game (4,10)
2. Led NHL in goals 2001, FL Pavel ___ (4)
4. 1999 Conn Smythe DAL, Joe ___ (10)
6. Flames mascot name (6)
8. 1994 Stanley Cup champs (3,4,7)
9. Vezina winner 2022 (4,10)
10. 1st player to have 100+ points in rookie season, 1981, Peter (7)
11. COL G, Darcy ___ (7)
15. 1945 NHL MVP, MTL, Elmer ___ (4)
17. 1970 Vezina winner, Tony ___ (8)
18. 2014 Vezina winner, Tuukka ___ (4)
20. Led NHL in goals 1986, Jari ___ (5)

Puzzle #39

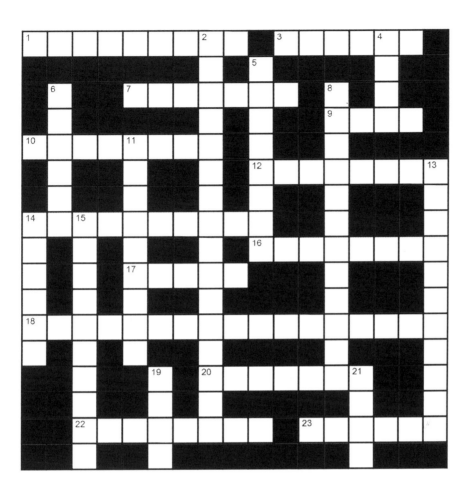

Across

1. To hit an opponent with your body, to block him or take him out of the play (4,5)
3. Another word for a great deke or pass (6)
7. 1955 NHL MVP, TOR, Ted _____ (7)
9. 1965 and 1966 NHL MVP, CHI, Bobby ___ (4)
10. Undrafted Flames all star, Mark _____ (8)
12. Light behind goal (3,5)
14. 1966 James Norris winner, Jacques _____ (10)
16. Shane Doan jersey number (8)
17. Bruins single season shooting % record Cam ____ (5)
18. 1991 Presidents' Trophy (7,10)
20. 1998 Conn Smythe DET, Steve ___ (7)
22. Led NHL in goals 2020, Pastrnak and (8)
23. Bruins (6)

Down

2. Vezina winner 2020 (6,10)
4. 1968 Conn Smythe, STL Glenn _____ (4)
5. Boston arena (2,6)
6. Led NHL in goals 2002, Jarome _____ (6)
8. Flyers (12)
11. CHI RW, Alex _____ (9)
13. Scott Niedermayer number (6,5)
14. 1994 Conn Smythe NYR, Brian ___ (6)
15. 2001 Conn Smythe COL (7,3)
19. Sabre with highest single season plus/minus, Don ____ (4)
21. Led NHL in goals 2004, COL Rick _____ (4)

Puzzle #40

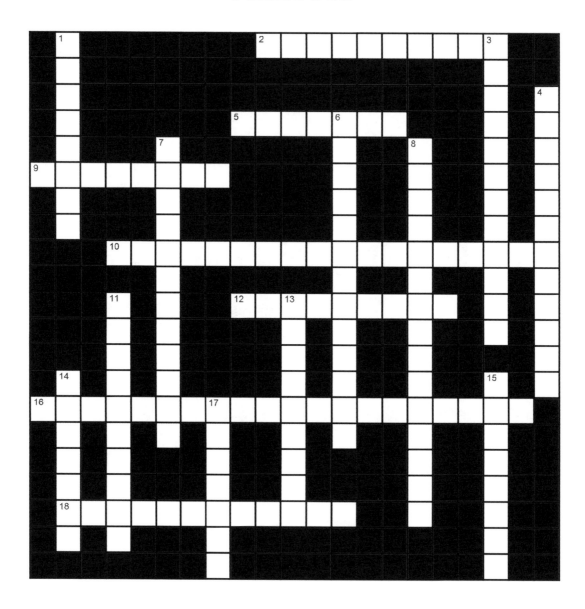

Across

2 1980 Winter Olympics location (4,6)

5 Doug's job in Goon (7)

9 Frederick Backman novel (8)

10 Total goals divided by shots taken (8,10)

12 2013 Vezina winner, Sergei _____ (9)

16 NHL (8,6,6)

18 Led NHL in goals 2009 (4,8)

Down

1 2022 NHL MVP, Auston ___ (8)

3 1994 Vezina winner, BUF (7,5)

4 Dallas Stars mascot (6,1,5)

6 Daniel Brière nickname (6,7)

7 2020 Presidents' Trophy (6,6)

8 1995 Stanley Cup champs (3,6,6)

11 Lost 2002 Stanley Cup to DET (10)

13 Checking an opponent while skating backward toward one's own goal (4,5)

14 Capitals captain 1982-1993, Rod _____ (7)

15 Georges Vezina nickname, Chicoutimi _____ (8)

17 1995 Conn Smythe NJ, Claude ____ (7)

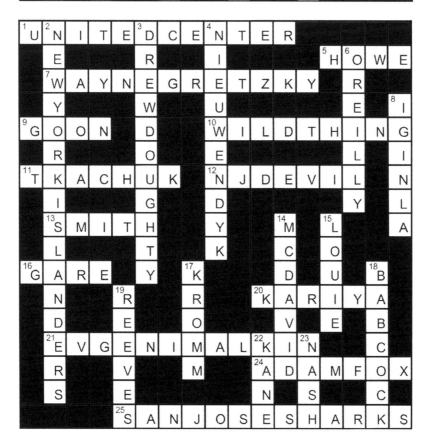

3

Across:
1. FRANKBRIMSEK
6. KELLY
8. DRAISAITL
11. LETANG
12. CHELIOS
16. MONTREALCANADIENS
18. GREEN
19. JONATHANQUICK

Down:
4. STAAL
5. CHARLIESIMMER

4

Across:
3. BRIMSEK
5. TROTZ
7. VULCANIZEDRUBBER
10. HONDACENTER
12. TAMPABAY
14. SHUTT
15. KRAKEN
18. WHALE
19. GORDIEHOWE
20. BRODA
21. EIGHTEEN
22. SANJOSE

Down:
1. DAVESCHULTZ

5

Puzzle grid answers:

Across: FACEOFF · SLAVIN · PREDATORS · SIDNEY CROSBY · BOBROVSKY · TAMPA BAY LIGHTNING · STEWART · DUNCAN KEITH · SHERO · BIG BEN · GOULET

Down (readable): FRANCIS

```
F A C E O F F . W . S L A V I N  N
R . E . . I . . H . U . . . . .  O
A . L . P R E D A T O R S . . .  R D
N . K . L . . L . . . . . . B .  .
C . Y . S I D N E Y C R O S B Y
I . . . . . R . . . N . . E . .
S . B O B R O V S K Y . M . R
. . B . . . . . . . . A . N
T A M P A B A Y L I G H T N I N G
R . A . N . . . E . T . . E
O . C . . H . . M . A . H . . . S
U . L . . U . . A . S T E W A R T
D U N C A N K E I T H . W . R . L
A . N . . T . . R . . . S H E R O
. B I G B E N . . E . . . . N . U
. . S . . . R . G O U L E T . . I
. . . . . . . . . . . . . . . . S
```

6

Puzzle grid answers:

Across: SHIFT · QUEBEC · RYAN OREILLY · SHORTHANDED GOAL · HOWE · CROSBY · GEOFFRION · HASEK · MICKE MOOSE · NIEDERMAYER · PUCK

Down (readable): SEDIN · CALGARY FLAMES

```
S H I F T . . . C . Q U E B E C
E . I . . . G . H . . . R . A
D . N . . R Y A N O R E I L L Y
I . T . . E . R . . . D . G
N . . S H O R T H A N D E D G O A L
. . . E . Z . . . . . E . R
. H O W E . K . . . C R O S B Y
B . H . . Y . D . H . T . F
R . A . . . . E . E . O . L
E . L . G E O F F R I O N . A
A . E . L . E . R . E . M
D . . H . B . N . Y . H A S E K
M I C K E M O O S E . S . R . S
A . . . J . W . E . T . E . . B
N . . . D . I . M . A . N . . U
. . . . U . N I E D E R M A Y E R
. P U C K . G . N . . S . . . E
```

7

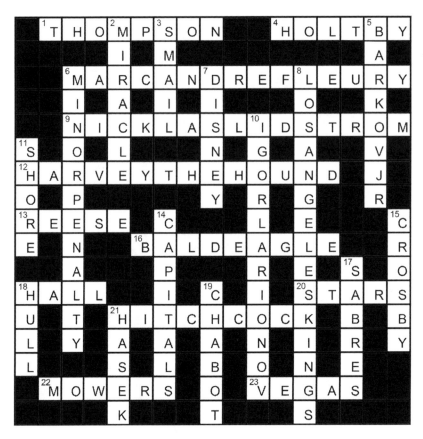

8

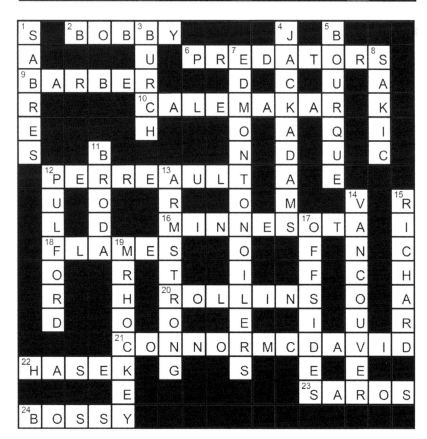

11

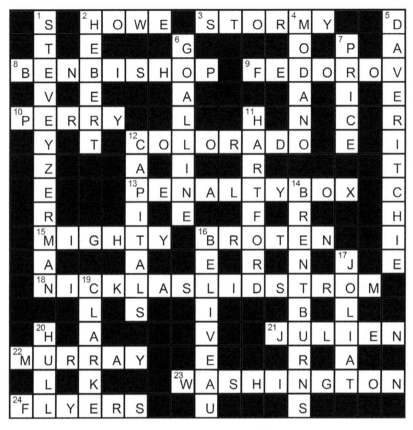

12

13

14

15

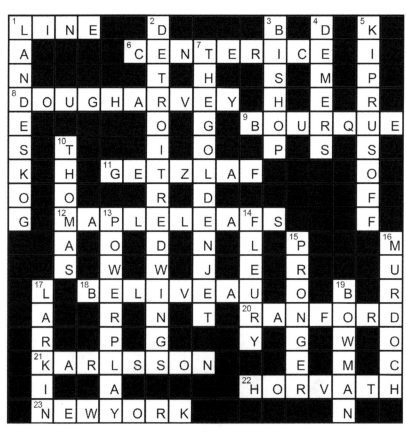

16

17

- 1 P
- 2 P
- 3 SCHEIFELE
- 4 CAPITALS
- 5 G
- 6 S
- 7 B
- 8 MONTREAL
- 9 VEZINA
- 10 PHOENIXCOYOTES
- 11 O
- 12 C
- 13 CASSIDY
- 14 BOSSY
- 15 S
- 16 TKACHUK
- 17 BERNIE
- 18 C
- 19 PRONGER
- 20 SABRES
- 21 HOOKING

Down column letters (left to right):
P-O-C-K-E-T-R-O-C-K-E-T (POCKETROCKET)
P-H-I-L-A-S-I-M-O-N (PHILASIMON)
S-E-A-L
M-O-N-T-R-E-A-L
G-A-L-A-G-E-B...
S-N-A-N-A-O-R
B-L-U-E-S

18

- 1 MAURICE
- 2 B
- 3 TESSIER
- 4 M
- 5 M
- 6 V
- 7 L
- 8 MINNESOTA
- 9 N
- 10 M
- 11 LOSANGELESKINGS
- 12 G
- 13 HAINSWORTH
- 14 H
- 15 LEMAIRE
- 16 HEDMAN
- 17 A
- 18 COUGARS
- 19 FLAMES
- 20 DRYDEN
- 21 CANUCKS
- 22 BELIVEAU

Down column letters (left to right):
M-I-K-E-M-I-L-B-U-R-Y (MIKEMILBURY)
B-A-L-L-A-R-R-R...
T-K-A-C-H-U-J-O
M-I-T-A-H-I-D-O
S-H-A-R-V-I-N-L-L-E-H-C
V-O-L-O-N-O-N
L-I-D-J-O-W-A-T-H-A
M-O-N-A-H-A-N
A-T-L-A-N-T

19

Across and Down entries (filled grid):

- 1 POKECHECK
- 6 GAUDREAU
- 7 HOWELL
- 8 RAYBOURQUE
- 9 PEETERS
- 13 CHICLETS
- 15 MESSIER
- 17 BRADRICHARDS
- 19 MACTAVISH
- 20 ALFREDSSON
- 21 SHORE
- 22 TOMMYHAWK

Down entries include:
- 1 PENGUINSTEWART
- 2 CARLYLE
- 3 COUTURIER
- 4 HAGGERTY
- 5 DALLASSTARS
- 10 SHHMHM
- 11 SHMHMD
- 12 LMIEUX
- 14 CANADARS
- 16 STEWART
- 18 STON

20

Across and Down entries (filled grid):

- 1 UMPIRES
- 4 MINNESOTA
- 6 PARENT
- 10 FORSBERG
- 12 OVECHKIN
- 15 SAINTPATRICK
- 17 FLAMES
- 19 DOUGHARVEY
- 21 DURNAN
- 22 PENGUINS
- 23 CHERRY
- 24 HISCHIER

Down entries include:
- 2 MCAVOY
- 3 GARDINER
- 5 SAWCHUCK
- 7 GIT
- 8 SCTST
- 9 THWCMU
- 13 COFFEY
- 14 ILVIVY
- 16 DEVILS
- 18 CLEY
- 20 MILLER

21

```
 1T  E  R  R  Y  S  A  W  C  H  U  K        2O     3K
 O                                           I      I
 4R  O  M  A  N  J  O  S  I        5M  U  L  L  E  N
 T                          6P              E      G
 O     7B     8J     9G  A  R  D  I  N  E  R     S
 R     O           10C           I              S
 E     N     Y        A           C        11V     12B
13L  A  D  Y  B  Y  N  G  M 14E  M  O  R  I  A  L
 L     R     E     U        A        G        U
15A  V  A  L  A  N  C  H  E    16P  R  O  N  G  E  R
             G     K           L        E     J
17P           L     S    18B  R  E  A  K  A  W  A  Y
19S  A  T  H  E  R        R     L     U        C
 R                 U        E     L           K
 E       20K  O  P  I  T  A  R        T        E
 N                 N        F                  T
 T       21B  U  R  N  S    22S  H  A  R  K  S
```

22

```
 1S 2M  I 3T  H        4S 5I  M  M  E  R              6T
 A     H           A           7Z           O
 8S  T  O  R  M  Y     9R  A  N  T  A  N  E  N
 C     E           I           M           W
 H     E       10C  O  L  U  M  B  U  S
 I       11K     O                 O        12S
13N  O  R  D  I  Q  U  E 14S        N           C
 G        L        T        W 15W  I  L 16S  O  N
17P  A  V  E  L  B  U  R  E           O        T
 E        E          18E  S  P  O  S  I  T  O
 N    19C  A  R  E  Y     P           A        S
 A     A              C           N        T
20L  I  N  D 21B  E  R  G  H    22H  U  G  H  E  S
 T     U     E           E           E        V
23V  I  N  C  E  N  T  L  E  C  A  V  A  L  I  E  R
 E     K     N           K              E     N
 S     S          24J  E  T  S              S
```

23

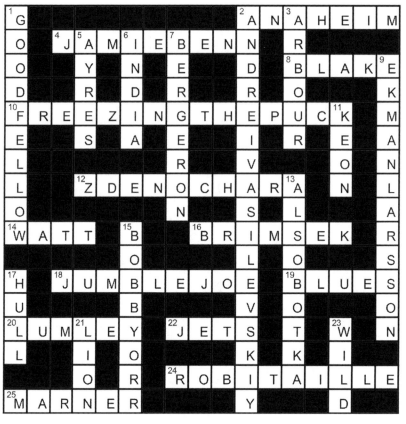

24

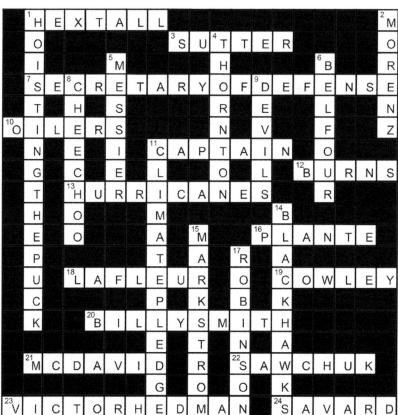

25

Across
- 1. BOWMAN
- 5. VANCOUVER CANUCKS
- 8. MIKITA
- 10. NEW YORK RANGERS
- 11. GAINEY
- 12. PARENT
- 14. BATHGATE
- 17. ST LOUIS BLUES
- 18. SLAPSHOT
- 19. CHELIOS
- 20. GRETZKY

Down (letters visible)
- 2. MAKINSON
- 3. SNATTRS...
- 4. ASTON
- 6. CLARRE
- 7. SPEAS...
- 9. MO GILLINNY
- 13. MESSII
- 15. GAH W
- 16. SUTTER

26

Across
- 3. MAPLE LEAFS
- 6. TONY ESPOSITO
- 7. LIDSTROM
- 8. CANADIENS
- 9. DALLAS STARS
- 11. DELAYED PENALTY
- 14. BAILEY
- 16. MESSIER
- 17. AVALANCHE
- 19. SHORE
- 20. HUNTER
- 21. KHUDOBIN
- 22. COURNOYER

Down (letters visible)
- 1. MOGILNY
- 2. JOHNSON
- 4. FLORSDE...
- 5. MNSE SO
- 10. MIKITA
- 12. PUCKTHRY
- 13. BELIVAAU
- 15. LAFLEUR
- 18. HOWLL

27

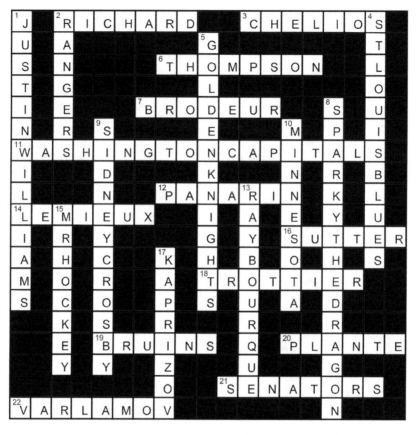

28

29

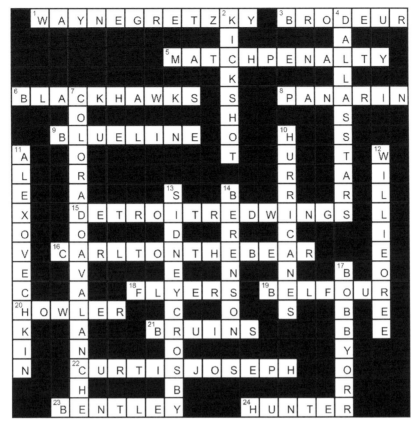

30

31

32

33

- 1 TRIPPING
- 2 PILL
- 3 VASILEVSKIY
- 6 STOUGHTON
- 10 SHORE
- 12 PROFLY
- 13 HASEK
- 15 MILLER
- 16 MADISONSQUAREGARDEN
- 20 MACLEAN
- 21 NORDY
- 22 BLUES
- 23 KEENAN
- 24 MARTIN

34

- 1 HATTRICK
- 7 ABEL
- 8 QUEBEC
- 9 TIPPETT
- 11 OTTAWA
- 12 GORDIEHOWE
- 13 SCOTIABANKARENA
- 16 MIKEMODANO
- 17 POINT
- 18 DALLAS
- 20 TEEMU
- 21 RODLANGWAY
- 22 PASTRNAK

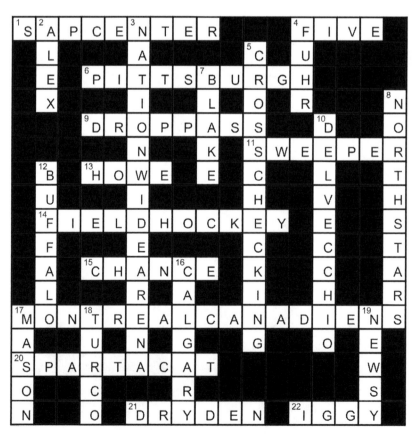

37

Across / entries:
- HALL
- EIGHT
- BUTTENDING
- NEWJERSEYDEVILS
- MAKAROV
- RAYNER
- WRISTSHOT
- BEAR
- ALIEN
- SABRETOOTH
- LAINE
- NOLAN
- KIPRUSOFF
- KANE
- ESPOSITO

Down / entries:
- ANIDING
- LILLARD
- BLLARU
- BUTLYSS
- THHARD
- MUELLER
- CRETTER
- COMCLELY
- SACBNE
- ALIEN
- LENNYBIII
- BNNY
- KISIINI
- YUSPOOL
- SHLO

38

Across / entries:
- GOALIE
- GNASH
- DOUG
- VANBIESBROUCK
- ELEVEN
- SIDNEYCROSBY
- MARCHAND
- KERR
- DEKE
- ALTHEOCTOPUS
- GARE
- RINNE
- POTVIN
- KARLSSON
- DETROIT

Down / entries:
- GAMEMI
- BREGWOA
- NIEHE
- HAA
- HIE
- LAMPLIGHDYE
- OCTGHYAR
- SVDRKER
- NELNDUCT
- KURR
- ESPOSITO
- RK

39

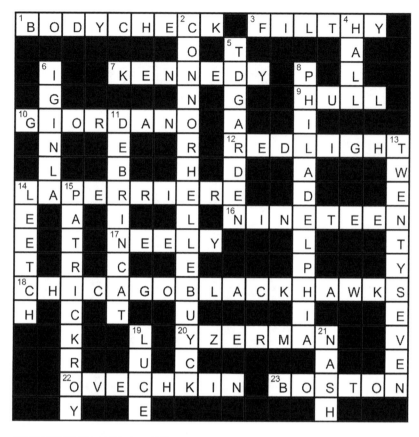

40

Made in United States
Troutdale, OR
12/12/2024

26345194R00035